TABLE OF CONTENTS

AUTHOR'S PAGE

Donna Proper is a seasoned writer and a child educator that writes different genres ranging from family,relationship, love, parenting, nutrition, career etc.

She's inspired to write this book ' The Greed in Man' due to her experience with people in the world who thinks they can acquire everything in the world thereby destroying themselves in the process.

Sit back, read and learn from this book. Don't forget to drop your review as well.
 Thanks.

INTRODUCTION TO GREED

(A) MEANING OF GREED

Greed is an intense and selfish desire for more wealth, power, or material possessions than one needs or deserves. It is a dangerous emotion that can lead to destructive behavior if not kept in check.
It is generally considered a negative emotion and is associated with immoral behavior.

Greed is a powerful motivator that drives people to acquire material possessions, wealth, and power. It can be a double-edged sword, as it can lead to success, but can also lead to unethical behavior and corruption.

Greed motivates people to work hard and strive for success, but can also lead to extreme selfishness and a disregard for the needs of others.

(B) MAN IS GREEDY

Mrs Williams is a successful businesswoman that deals
in clothing and fashion accessories. She also does

Catering and Decoration. Some months she makes serious money, other months might be dry due to low patronage but all in all, she's comfortable. Her husband is not doing badly for himself and he

takes care of most of the family's needs. Mrs Williams always complains about her business and the fact that she wants to make more money and you will always see her engaging in different online businesses both genuine and ingenuine ones. Her husband always warns her to stick to her primary business that's thriving gradually but she won't have any of that.

One day Mrs Williams saw one business opportunity online which requires her to put little money and earn profit without doing anything stressful other than clicking one or two things and following the instructions given. She started making little profits and was withdrawing them into her account. It seemed too good to be true. She kept at it and at a point she started making serious profit after she was asked each time to increase her initial capital with them. The higher the capital, the higher the profit. She spent all her money on this online business and didn't stop there. She started borrowing from family and friends so she can execute the big tasks given to her and withdraw the big profit she will make. She asked to borrow some money from her husband but the husband declined and warned her to be careful. She didn't listen and went ahead to borrow money from her sister-in-law promising to send it in a few hours. Immediately she completed this big task gulping millions of dollars, but her account was not credited with the profit. She tried withdrawing the money but it kept declining. She contacted the customer service representatives who told her to do some more tasks so she can be credited with everything. When she kept disturbing him, her line was blocked.

There and then, she realised she had been duped. She remembered how her husband warned her severally against the business. She went into depression because she lost millions of dollars. She's owing several debts and her main business folded up.

Man is a creature driven by greed, a desire for more than what he already has. We live in a world where we are constantly trying to acquire more money, power, or influence. We may use our resources to help those in need, but we often find ourselves with a desire to have more than we currently have. We may not even be aware of our greed, but it often manifests itself in our decisions and actions. Greed can lead to a variety of negative consequences, such as increasing stress and anxiety levels, creating financial instability, and damaging relationships. It can also lead to unethical or illegal behaviour in an attempt to gain or maintain power. Greed can be a destructive force, but it can also be used to motivate us to achieve our goals. By recognizing our greed, we can make better decisions that will benefit both ourselves and those around us.

Greed is one of the factors affecting several nations of the world. The ruling class wants the whole masses to be under them and their children, hence they hold on to power and keep circulating it amongst themselves. Men keep acquiring wealth (through unhealthy means) that they can't exhaust themselves keeping them for their unborn generations. The desire to have more than others keep man wanting more and more, making him insatiable and destroying others in the process of acquiring wealth.

TYPES OF GREED

(A) FINANCIAL GREED

Financial greed is an excessive desire to acquire or possess more money or wealth than one needs. It can motivate people to behave irresponsibly or unethically in pursuit of financial gain. Greed can lead to unethical practices such as bribery, fraud, insider trading and other forms of corruption. It can also put individuals and organizations at risk of financial losses, legal action and public backlash. Ultimately, financial greed can have a damaging effect on the economy as a whole.

The only way to combat financial greed is to create a culture of responsible financial management and ethical behavior. Individuals and organizations should strive to be transparent and accountable in their financial dealings. They should also be aware of the risks associated with excessive greed, and take steps to ensure that they are exercising sound judgement when making financial decisions. Finally, individuals should strive to be content with what they have and focus on creating long-term financial stability rather than short-term gain.

(B) GREED FOR POWER

Greed for power is an unhealthy and destructive force that can lead to negative consequences for individuals, groups, and societies. It is the desire to gain and maintain control over others and can manifest in numerous ways, such as bullying, intimidation, and manipulation. Greed for power can lead to a breakdown of trust and respect, as well as a lack of collaboration and team work. It can lead to the exploitation of people, resources, and situations in order to benefit oneself or those in one's inner circle. Ultimately, unchecked greed for power can lead to a culture of fear and oppression and can have far-reaching and long-lasting damaging effects.

© GREED FOR KNOWLEDGE

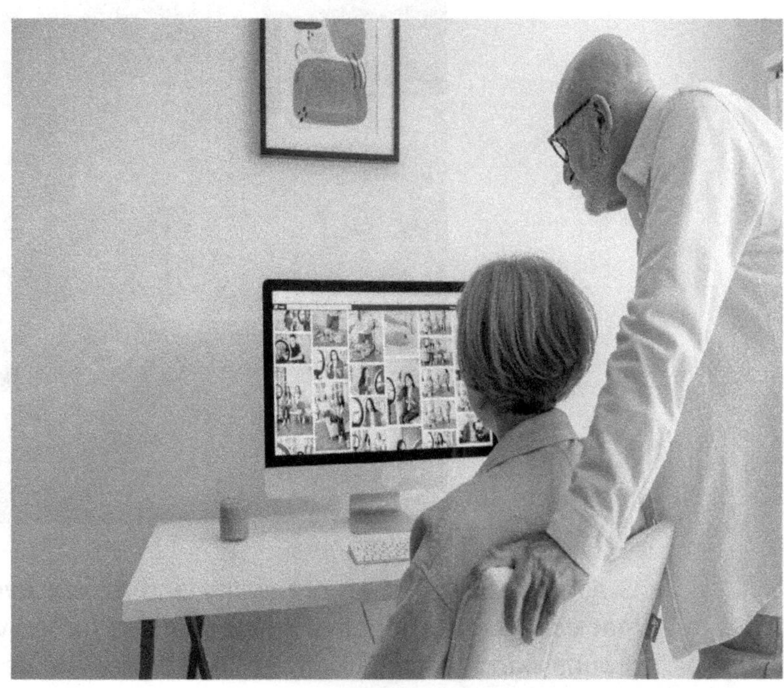

Greed for knowledge is the desire to learn more and gain new skills without any external motivation. It is driven by an internal motivation to understand and grow intellectually. This type of greed is not necessarily a bad thing; it can often be beneficial as it encourages people to find innovative solutions to problems and develop new skills.

Greed for knowledge can be seen in successful people who never seem to stop learning. They are always looking for new challenges and opportunities to grow and develop. They are motivated by their own curiosity and satisfaction of learning something new. It can also be seen in those who are constantly seeking out new information and experiences, in an effort to strengthen their knowledge and skills.

(D) GREED FOR MATERIAL POSSESSIONS

Greed for material possessions has become a major problem in our society. . People are driven by the need to acquire as many material goods as possible, even if it means going into debt or sacrificing important aspects of life such as health, relationships, and spiritual pursuits. This unchecked desire for material goods has caused an overall decrease in the quality of life and well-being for many individuals. It can also lead to increased stress, a feeling of never being satisfied, and even depression. To combat this problem, individuals should strive to focus on the things that truly matter in life such as relationships, spirituality, and personal growth. Additionally, it is important to become aware of advertising and marketing tactics that often encourage us to purchase goods we don't need. By understanding the root causes of our desire for material possessions, we can work towards a more balanced lifestyle.

(E) GREED IN RELIGION

Greed in religion refers to the phenomenon of people using religious beliefs and practices to further their own selfish interests. This can involve people taking advantage of their positions in religious organizations for financial or personal gain, or it can refer to people using religion to manipulate others or exploit their faith for their own gain. Greed in religion can also involve people using religious beliefs or practices to control or oppress others. Greed in religion can have a damaging effect on individuals, communities, and societies, and is often seen as a form of corruption.

GREED IN MODERN SOCIETY

Greed is a common problem in modern society, as people seek to acquire wealth and possessions at all costs. The prevalence of greed can be seen in the way people are willing to pay exorbitant amounts of money to acquire items that they do not need or use, while others struggle to make ends meet. Greed can also be seen in the way corporations and businesses prioritise profits over ethical considerations, leading to exploitation of workers, environmental damage and excessive accumulation of goods. Greed can also be found in the way in which people use their influence and power to gain more wealth and power. Greed can lead to a culture of inequality and can be seen in the widening gap between the wealthy and the poor. Ultimately, greed has the potential to corrode society, as it leads to a lack of empathy, a lack of compassion, and selfishness.

CAUSES OF GREED IN HUMANS

1. **Fear of scarcity**: Humans often develop an attitude of greed when they fear that resources or opportunities are limited. They, therefore, want to keep accumulating so they don't lack at any time. Some time ago, in some African countries, it was revealed that a lot of cash running to millions was stashed away in different places.

Most of the cash had been destroyed by moisture or insects. They were discovered when there was a need for the country to change its currency.

2. **Unchecked ambition**: Greed can be a result of an individual's ambition to acquire more than what is necessary or appropriate. How do you explain old men and women in politics holding on to power for too long even when they're physically drained.

3. **Social pressure**: Greed is often fueled by the desire to keep up with others or to be better than them. Most people want to be above others so they can be in control of others at their will.

4. **Lack of self-control**: Greed can also be a result of an individual's inability to control their impulses and desires. Greed has taken the better part of some people so much so they can't control their appetite to have more even if they will cut corners. A good example is the story in the introduction page where Mrs Williams wants to acquire more money not minding whether the business she's engaging in is legal or not.

5. **Desire for power**: Greed is often linked to a desire for power and control over others and resources. This one is affecting most developing nations in the world where the old hold on to power and refuse to let go of the younger generation. The fame, prestige, power and affluence attached to elective positions made most

leaders desire power and are ready to pay any price to get there by all means.

6. **Unmet needs**: Greed can often be a result of unmet needs and a desire to fulfil those needs extremely. So many needs to be met so man naturally looks for several ways to meet them. Some even go to the extent of engaging in rituals, killings, robbery, stealing etc to meet their needs. Some ladies engage in prostitution just to meet their needs. Others steal government funds to meet their needs. The list is endless.

7. **Lack of empathy**: Greed can also be a result of a lack of empathy and understanding for others. Man mostly uses what he has to get what he wants not minding the consequences. Some kill others to meet their needs. Others steal funds meant for others because of greed in them. Greed has made some leaders not care for their subordinates, they care about themselves alone and care less about those under them.

8. **Greed as a coping mechanism**: Greed can also be used as a coping mechanism to deal with difficult and painful experiences.

9. **Disregard for the environment**: Greed can also be a result of a disregard for the environment and its resources.

10. **Poor role models**: Greed can be perpetuated by poor role models or other individuals who demonstrate and encourage greedy behaviour. Greed is gradually becoming a norm in society. The younger generations are seeing the older generations how they are amazing wealth to themselves and cheating others to get to the top by cutting corners. The younger generations too are mapping out strategies to outshine the older generations. The older generations use analog methods to cheat and steal, the younger generations are planning their strategies using digital and technology to steal. This explains the high rate of digital crime in the world now. This is because they're more informed.

EFFECTS OF GREED ON HUMAN

Greed can have several destructive effects on man which include:-

-**Lack of Trust**:   It can lead to a lack of trust and cooperation, creating a hostile and competitive environment.

- **Self- Interest**: It can also cause people to act out of self-interest without regard for the consequences, leading to unethical and even illegal behavior. Greed makes man think of himself alone without thinking of the consequences of his illegal actions to others.

-**Short-Term Gain**: Greed can also lead to a focus on short-term gain and a disregard for long-term growth, leading to a lack of sustainability and a potential for significant losses. Greed can make man to loose all he has in his bid to acquire more through illegal means. A good example is Mrs Williams' story in the introduction.

- **Inequality**: Finally, greed can create a cycle of inequality, as those with more resources can take advantage of those with less.
- **Impoverished Nation**: Greed will make a nation to be in abject poverty as the masses will be subjected to suffering and pain since the collective wealth of the nation is been enjoyed by the few that are in power.
- **Sickness/ Death**: Greed can lead to sickness of the greedy one or even death in a few cases. A greedy person might one day loose all and this might lead to depression which can cause severe sickness. If this sickness is not well managed, it can lead to death.

STRATEGIES TO OVERCOME GREED IN HUMAN

1. **Acknowledge Greed:** The first step in overcoming greed is to recognize that it exists and be honest with yourself about how it has affected your decisions.

2. **Set Realistic Goals:** Greed is often caused by unrealistic expectations. Make sure your goals are achievable and focus on the long-term to avoid becoming too greedy. Stop expecting too much or get-rich syndrome. Set achievable goals within your means.

3. **Practice Gratitude:** Greed is often caused by a lack of appreciation for what we already have. Cultivate an attitude of gratitude for the good things in your life.

4. **Cultivate Generosity:** Generosity is the opposite of greed. Practicing generosity by giving of your time and money to counteract the urge to be greedy. It's always better to give than to receive.

5. **Cultivate Contentment:** Contentment is the antidote to greed. Learn to be content with what you have and to be happy with the life you have.

6. **Find Healthy Ways to Spend Money:** Greed often comes from a desire to buy things that we don't need. Find healthy ways to spend money and invest in experiences or activities that bring you joy.

7. **Avoid Temptations:** Greed can be caused by temptations. Avoid situations or activities that trigger your greed and replace them with more positive activities. Stop comparing yourself with others. Always note that you will always meet people that have more than you.

8. **Develop Self-Awareness:** Developing a better understanding of yourself and your emotions can help to identify when greed is taking over.

9. **Reach Out for Help:** If you feel like you are struggling to overcome greed, don't hesitate to reach out for help from a friend, family member, or professional.

10. **Practice Mindfulness:** Mindfulness can help to cultivate awareness and acceptance and prevent us from getting caught up in greed.

CONCLUSION

Greed is a powerful emotion that can lead to a great deal of suffering and harm. It can cause people to act in ways that are destructive and unethical, leading to a range of negative consequences. Greed can also lead to a lack of empathy and compassion for others, which can have a detrimental impact on our relationships and society as a whole.

Greed can cause people to act in ways that are unethical, selfish, and dishonest. It can lead to corruption, exploitation, and a lack of empathy or compassion for others. Greed often leads to a distorted sense of priorities and can cause people to put their own needs first, regardless of the consequences for others. Greed can also lead to a feeling of never being satisfied with what one has, no matter how much they have.

In short, greed is an emotion that can have devastating consequences and should be avoided at all costs. It is important to remember that having more than one needs does not necessarily make one happier, and that it is important to be content with what one has. Greed can lead to an obsession with material possessions and an unhealthy focus on money, which can lead to a lack of appreciation for the simpler things in life.

Ultimately, it is important to remember that greed can be managed and controlled, and that it is possible to lead a life that is free from its destructive influence.